These Flowers were held by Broken Vases

William James Lofton Jackson

These Flowers were held by Broken Vases

cover art by willette lofton

you are a gem.

These Flowers were held by Broken Vases

to those who Love me,

to those who could not Love me as i needed them to,

and to those who will try and fail, **thank you**.

this is only possible because of you.

note from the author

this is my truth. These Flowers were held by Broken Vases is the rising and falling of injury; from raw flesh to scar tissue. each poem is a victory flag. each line is a conquered battle. this work pivots across the dance floor of when parents play with matches around their children, fouettes fiercely into the ballroom of racial injustice and lands on scraped knees toward the altars of healing. in life there will be moments where we entrust people with loving us entirely, without hesitation and many will drop the ball. this is neither a reflection of your worth nor is it a reflection of who they are as a person. we are flawed creations, but nonetheless we are beautiful flowers. we have clawed our way through the soil of disappointment and have erupted into a life full of second chances, hope, and Love.

Love is never failing, for it conquers all.

shatter

: to break suddenly into many small pieces

These Flowers were held by Broken Vases

these flowers will be rotten in a couple hours. birds will crap on them. the smoke here will make them stink, and tomorrow a bulldozer will probably run over them, but for right now they are so beautiful.

−chuck palahniuk

baptism

people are not bath water

you do not have the privilege to be immersed in them,

wash the filth from your flesh and leave them when you have turned them cold

hand out short-ended sticks and expect thank you cards just for showing up

showing up and actually being there are two different destinations

your legacy is a kingdom of dirty bathtubs

and

skeletons with the gristle and parcels of meat still attached

These Flowers were held by Broken Vases

how much dynamite have you velcroed to your palms?

ran your hands over shea butter flesh just to detonate innocence into accusation

how does *it* feel?

to have made oceans out of mountains, memories out of Lovers

people are not occasional sunsets,

only available when you decide their beauty is worth admiring

how does *it* feel to dress yourself in suicide vests and arming your tongue with silver?

people are not your bath water,

they are not the towel to dry you of your sin

These Flowers were held by Broken Vases

home alone

i wonder if my bones could have ever been more eternity than christmas-time satisfactory

could your palms have Loved me enough to pray me through pacific ocean tidal waves?

could the mother

could the father, buried in the coffins of chests

Love me pass street corners and onto the dean's list

or to board ships set to sail for scholars the color of africa's shadow

were there sunday suppers stored in the pantries of your soul?

we aint got much to eat 'round here

but hell,

These Flowers were held by Broken Vases

nothing a lil scripture and cornbread can't fix

could your fingers turn the tassels to all these seasons i've had to spring through to keep from falling?

i never cared about making sunsets stutter to see my smile,

i wouldn't fear holidays because home would be anywhere your arms would catch me

you caught me,

caught me wishing for possibilities

let's be realistic

if you were here

there wouldn't be busted pipes in my eyes,

or

a gas leak in my heart

i wouldn't have abandonment issues

These Flowers were held by Broken Vases

i wouldn't fear God walking out on me...

These Flowers were held by Broken Vases

└ *hurting me*

strike the match down my sternum

drag it over every single rib

create a horizon out of me

you know i will be here/the sweat still evaporating from the last time you made me swallow the sun

soon my stomach will be a titanium park with tungsten swings and monkey bars

organs should never transform into factories

loving you reminds me of the war stories grandpa told me

it took everything from him/left scars in places eyes are too scared to look at

and dared to call him a survivor

These Flowers were held by Broken Vases

he tore up his draft card one day

but he never turned in his combat boots

i do not want to be like him.

These Flowers were held by Broken Vases

∟ **restless**

i gave you **all** of me

everything...

pulled the **breath** & the **heart** out of me

unlocked my fences/left the door pushed up/**not closed**...

kept the lamp on, so you would not stumble in the darkness

dinner was in the oven, bath water had grown **cold** waiting for *you*

i have grown **cold** waiting for you

has the **fire** gone out for me?

i looked for a goodbye note under your pillow/found **nothing** but coolness/coldness/emptiness

These Flowers were held by Broken Vases

searched the closet/found **sadness**

kitchen/i still set the table for **two**

showers/ i should not have to coach myself out of **drowning**

i gave you all of **me**

even the parts i do not show the mirror/still managed to **crack**

no matter how much we try/we still manage to **crack**

can you help me forget you/ **unteach** this butterfly of its wings?

teach the **coldness** to forget how to hold

These Flowers were held by Broken Vases

L the night you made me remember my mother

my mother told me one morning,

after she had finished playing in the snow

God had fashioned my smile and crocheted my sadness using

beethoven's symphony no.9

i laughed in d minor

she said/son, some people will be deaf to the music of you,

sometimes even yourself/

there are harps,

violins,

cellos

gathered in holy assembly,

strings vibrating in praise

These Flowers were held by Broken Vases

celebrating the capillaries carrying oxygen to your

heart

brain

...you are breathing

Love is not a soundproof room

she said/never blame yourself for the slow infirmity that deafens people to the vinyl records lining your gums

everyone is not efficacious in the way of appreciating smiles, ignorant to the religion of closing eyelids and breathing deeply and loving what's in front of them without hesitation/

this entire tiding, she declared in a mudslide of slurred words and half closed eyes

she must not have understood that cocaine causes auditory hallucinations

maybe she heard something that was never truly there.

These Flowers were held by Broken Vases

foolish

what made me think this flesh be strong enough

be pure enough, be christ-like enough to

sacrifice my heart in return for heartbreak

where did i get the audacity to pull back my skin,

fold down my ribs and to expose my heart

i denied that you dressed yourself in

disappointment,

perfumed your palms with fallacious welcomes

taught your body to mold around mines and make

it feel real

i told God to quiet down when he sent warning,

told him i didn't care about being whole if i could

lay broken beside you

… shattered glass will always make you bleed if

not handled with care

what made me believe that i could be superman

and save you when you were driving in your

These Flowers were held by Broken Vases

lowest lane,

stand in front of freight trains

stop bullets from entering your picture frame...

i hold your picture at night in prayer and asks

God if he can forgive me of this sin,

is he sure that he doesn't have one more band –

aid with my name on it

these scratches feel like fire ant bites in

summer,

these broken pieces in my chest shake like

church bells reminding me that God is still there

even in the midst of pain

These Flowers were held by Broken Vases

∟ geometry, grammar, & God

my bones never asked to be a construction site for your soul to

live in

every piece of your smile

soaked within the circumference of my eyes

i whispered a prayer, hoping that no one but God would hear

me

yet you placed every

vowel

&

consonant

into your chest

treasured my pain even if it proved to only have value to me

These Flowers were held by Broken Vases

i warned you there was no profit in loving spilled milk

eternity had no room for us at its table

forever does not have enough napkins to keep cleaning up our mess

i don't want to keep making you feel like you're loving *a mess*

i'm sorry for causing this mess

These Flowers were held by Broken Vases

mother drowned

january 5th.

the rain made itself known/a stranger extending a greeting you should be hesitant to indulge

cold upon my flesh,

yet every bone in my body grinded together with the fiery after effects of death,

i had not died, yet i could not hear the hum of my heartbeat

my eyes watered, feeling sadness for my hands

they could not push God's decision into reverse

what happens when you try to arm wrestle with God?

that night, my heart unraveled and i witnessed pain pour like pebbles on an unkempt beach

sorrow tucked me in

These Flowers were held by Broken Vases

grief was my blanket

no solace came

just the kind of numbness that can be burned away by a shot of liquor

january 5th.

the day i asked God if he ever questions himself

the day i questioned a savior that told everyone he could walk on water…

- why didn't Jesus save my mama from drowning?

These Flowers were held by Broken Vases

father got lost on his way home

i could begin this poem by using your absent father as a punchline

but aint nothing funny about a clown that can't make a smile appear on his own child's face

aint nothing comic book appropriate about finding dust and shadows in your father's closet when all you were looking for was his superman cape

you are a walking ocean,

overflowing at the brim

if i was to cut your heart from your chest ,place it on the altar

would it testify that suicidal thoughts are side-effects of an absent father not teaching you to throw your shoulders back before entering any room?

see, the jokes are band-aid funny in elementary

These Flowers were held by Broken Vases

even in middle school, the hurt can be placed neatly in the back of your mind

high school *"yo good fa nothing daddy"* jokes feel like walking barefoot over a land-mine

splinters your ankles in half,

it pulls back every layer of *"i'm okay"*

absence boldly sits in the front row of your graduation

this pain hurts

you are more than comic relief

your inheritance is not found in the faults of your father

there is a gospel fluttering in your lungs

sing your soul free…

forgive your father for not having the courage to stay

…some blessings are better off not seen

forgive him for not being what you needed him to be

These Flowers were held by Broken Vases

These Flowers were held by Broken Vases

poets at 12:46 a.m.

every single promise you handed me

had expiration dates

grenades

and an assortment of Molotov cocktails

dangling dangerously from them

attempting to convince me that you had enough substance in your soul to cherish good company

you could not value me

 you reconciled for trying to place a price on my Love, paying bare minimum

you searched vigorously for the strings that would make my arms move away from guarding my heart/ forced me to watch as you created a crime scene out of my skin

These Flowers were held by Broken Vases

it was your goal to make me familiar with the pain our parents warn us about

the type of destruction that is decorated behind beautifully blossoming smiles and intentions camouflaged with the appearance of wanting to be Loved

you did not want to be Loved; you desired to be saved

...who stepped inside of your soul and placed bombs in places where my hands would reach

Innocent fingers blown into fragments

...who made you bleed so badly that you needed to share it

...who made you boycott Love ⁄

And why did you force me to participate in this sit-in

These Flowers were held by Broken Vases

⌊ frame me

caption this

attempting to neatly place the depth of our being into words

hoping that we have convinced our audience that we are more than vain headshots and insecurities wrapped handsomely into 612 pixels

yet so full of emptiness, socially provocative backgrounds become necessary

praying to God, bold in our vanity

that our crush, will not crush our heart

praying

saying

"i hope that i can crop out the pain

manipulate the mayfair, rise, or earlybird

to color

These Flowers were held by Broken Vases

to cover

who i really am"

subjecting ourselves to every filter, except God's refining fire

found in his Love, his word

using every filter/except normal

caption this…

These Flowers were held by Broken Vases

∟ house party

backs braced against the wall,

watching these daughters dance like stories around a campfire

fingers so full of empty things

red solo cups & people that will present themselves as fuzzy memories

preparing more for hangovers than homework

songs serenading these sacrifices we are making

the more we jig, our limbs

lock

pop

dislocate like twigs/waiting to become brush fire

who's sharing the bed with us and our loneliness tonight

being alone is a foreign language that makes us stop and stutter in our steps

These Flowers were held by Broken Vases

backs are braced against the wall/drink in hand

there is a beauty in wearing our skin like wrapping paper

& not a constitution of our freedom

ladies aint looking for liberty tonight

blunts rotating

rendering reels like stilled movies/Black & white cinemas

pure theatrics

for we know not our names/only these roles we play

this place is too dark to see which smiles really want to be here

these walls booming with the sound of a party that will leave most unsure if they are cool enough to be here

we find ourselves trying to recognize those we showed and gave everything to last night/it wasn't much

but it was everything we had

These Flowers were held by Broken Vases

all for someone who looks different in the sun/can't even smell you on them anymore

These Flowers were held by Broken Vases

L you made me say goodbye

your sun sidestepped from my sight

sopranoed a song that sounded off with the bells of separation

some pinkies are too weak to hold the anvil of a promise

sinners smiling

the toothpaste of sainthood painted on the enamel of their teeth

but the root is rotten as the corpses their mother has to bury from their father's closet

my soul cannot body bag your empty promises

aint a thing free fixed to the folding chair where disappointment sits and crosses its legs

aint a thing numbing enough to ignore pain

my bones can recite the language of farewells and can hum a hymn buzzing with the string of grief

These Flowers were held by Broken Vases

i Loved you because my fingers did not know how to hold the heaviness of my own brokenness

These Flowers were held by Broken Vases

└ apologetic

i folded memories of you origami style underneath my eyelids

i would see the beauty of who you were, even in my dreams

never would have guessed regret had fingers

trained to pluck every chord of nostalgia cradled between your

heart and your mind

you left me nothing but apologies

and i picked them up

tailored them to fit me

sat them down in my soul

wore them,

until i became one….

These Flowers were held by Broken Vases

L season greetings

i have witnessed generations of malice manipulate the mind and the heart of my family

vicious vices fixed and folded into the fingertips of a family fumbling to find ways to Love without breaking,

without leaving bruises and hearts carrying around Blacked eyes

ornaments at christmas have transformed into bombs

thrown with the intention to grenade Loved-ones apart at their seams

war has been waging

so many casualties have fell victim to this genocide, this civil war composed of brothers and sisters

holidays are seasonal,

These Flowers were held by Broken Vases

dysfunction delivers throughout the entire year

we bury secrets the color of charcoal

but there are some things and some people that do not satisfy the effects of pressure

…even patience can't wait for certain diamonds to develop

These Flowers were held by Broken Vases

L pulse

there are no beds in here or open closet doors\no plug-in night light searching for fireflies to fill its stomach

mother, i am having a hard time understanding where this monster came from

i am having a hard time understanding how bodies around me transformed into shattered bulbs\their flesh unmoving and bearing no warmth\their blood\a filament without voice

this bathroom smells like fear

the urinals are crying for *us*\God are you crying for us

or with us

mom, i'm scared

my heart feels like the rind of an orange\my eyes are too ripe to be picked like this

These Flowers were held by Broken Vases

mommy, where are the police\is my guardian angel scared of assault rifles too

no one taught me to die like this\i can't believe i'm going to die *like this*

if this is a thunderstorm\maybe i'm the rainbow

dedicated to the Pulse Nightclub victims

These Flowers were held by Broken Vases

people like us

walking passed

eyes averted

keeping our secret closed behind a smooth composure

i know we are both melting on the inside

secrets, sex, and sin tend to have that effect on people
wanting to touch things that are poisonous but taste like innocence

i am with my friends

you are with yours

flashes of last night tiptoe across my mind

i still smell you

the ghost of your breath visiting my skin

These Flowers were held by Broken Vases

it was a war torn field /filled and felt by fingers gripping at flesh

a dance of desperation

shoes kicked off

pants shift to our ankles like apologies ready to be forgiven

this is what it feels like to win the lottery

we walk pass each other, feeling the fire from last night burning in our chests

urban saints hooded in Black to hide our sin, our satisfaction

who knew that these nobodies could know bodies

but until tonight...

we do not know each other

These Flowers were held by Broken Vases

L abuser

how do you pretend as if you do not make people hold their laughter as if holding their breath

you push their smiles down their throat

wear latex gLoves to hide you were there

disemboweling a person's joy has become a mastered craft for you

scalpel flesh from chest

dig a cavity around their heart

pull the organ out

suture the wound back up

kiss them out of anesthesia,

...they never consented to this robbery.

These Flowers were held by Broken Vases

road, rings & reason

she begged for a ring and thought that his last name was a one-size-fits-all life jacket

girl, your burdens are too heavy to be buoyed by some boy that still confuses you for an option and not an opportunity to create magic with

some wizards just hide behind the curtains of their ego/nothing but smoke and mirrors

cannot truly give you anything you desire

find another yellow brick road to conquer, to click your heels on

i know that you're comfortable loving on the floor because you cannot fall from there,

 but that is not home dorothy

is there an underground railroad for girls like you?

These Flowers were held by Broken Vases

for hearts serving sentences to sojourners whom possess no truth worth salvaging

can harriet teach you how to part seas out of slavery and romance fantasies

can she teach you to create train tracks with your bare feet and get the hell on

blossom into a truth that will not be compromised

heartache is a language you are all too fluent in,

articulate in annunciating all the right syllables in sedition

queen, your heart has rehearsed more riot scenes than summers in the inner city of chicago

his intentions will never be strong enough to leave footprints on the moon

he can only photoshop himself into meeting your expectations

These Flowers were held by Broken Vases

his arms are not strong enough to hold your world together when it's crumbling

you are not meant to live alone

but every man you encounter will not be able to turn this house into a home

when you find yourself climbing the stairs,

turning the key

please do not be searching for him

...he does not know the art of Loving without intention

you are free to Love beyond the wrapping paper of empty people

dismissing God

you knocked on the door,

God blew out the lights…

i fought through the darkness,

bumped into chairs

ignored these beckons to sit

my fingers found the knob

i twisted it/it only turned halfway

my guardian angel wanted to unplug its halo and take a smoke break

i am no good with warning signs

i laugh at caution tape

These Flowers were held by Broken Vases

i do not wear sunglasses

- i am blinded by the smallest glare

i unlocked the door and managed to convince myself the hinges needed oil and it wasn't God moaning

i wonder how heavy the weight of breaking God's heart is / my arms are insignificant in length

you stood there, smelling of smoke

soot sat underneath the ledges of your fingernails

even then

i did not want to believe you had a thing for starting fires

...the kind where no one survives.

These Flowers were held by Broken Vases

L clark kent

it's sad

it's sad that you go so hard for him

and the only way he can show you how "hard" he goes for you is when he undoes his zipper

you're still painting pictures of him as your prince,

but cinderella, he is not the one in possession of your glass slipper

you have tricked yourself into thinking that with each stroke he takes

he's one stroke closer to be[cum]ing your ideal man

but he's like the little train

always saying "*i think i can, i think i can*"

but never does

These Flowers were held by Broken Vases

he hasn't realized that Love isn't a mid-grade drug and his emotions can't fit into a dime bag

so stop trying to rent out the vacant spaces in his heart

he never wanted to be your superman, that's why he settled for being just clark

These Flowers were held by Broken Vases

⌊ a captain is crying

it's a painful sight to see

watching your limbs turn into broken rainbows

...these promises do not offer gold at the finish line

ears demolished from being bunkers into bus stops for ballistic missiles

were we so naïve to believe that war zones only had legs

firsthand we have seen it fix its spine with wings of a c-17

the war came home with you

more than the residue of sand dusted your combat boots

i'm sorry that we could not grant you a peace treaty for your mind,

there are some deployments that last longer than nine months

bombs bellowing for Love too!

These Flowers were held by Broken Vases

death desiring for a soldier to sacrifice more than just his time

it's painful to see

flowers withering away

to witness their stems crinkle from the desert's heat

even the strongest heroes need help going to sleep

because ptsd is a lullaby that can slip a pill into your drink

make you dizzy and depressed

and have you wondering,

was it worth putting those boots on your feet?

colonel koon: *"it's always worth it…all you can do is Love each other."*

for cpt. andres schloemann

These Flowers were held by Broken Vases

⌊ burying myself

your voice can still a hummingbird's wings

bend feathers/whisper flight frozen

|gravity|

you make me realize there is such a thing as being held down and not knowing it

you swallow the sun in the morning/the moon is your supper

all the light of the world is being digested by you

we, rotate around which way your lips crease/hug our knees to our chest

summon prayers out of sadness which melts into anger

why are we so angry

why are we so damn angry

the man i was and the man i am now

this has become a sweet poison

These Flowers were held by Broken Vases

a burning with fire and a healing with aloe and honey

this morning i asked God to whisper hummingbirds and Black holes free

These Flowers were held by Broken Vases

there's something vulgar about being honest

father was never viewed as a righteous man

not even a right-ish kinda man

nor was he ever invited into his children's prayers at night

he proved that monsters are not interested in closets but they sit judas-style quiet at the head of dinner tables

with eyes the color of rape and a smile that crinkles and cracks with the stench of *"you betta not tell ya mutha"*

he Blacked her eyes during the day

she used this as her excuse to be blind at night

he always seemed to knock the rescue from her hands

she fumbled your lives so many times and couldn't find the courage to slit that bastard's throat

he burdened you with a crown no child should ever have to wear

These Flowers were held by Broken Vases

this is not how disney movies look

cinderella never had to give up more than a glass slipper to sleep at night

mother says she didn't know that father was a thief obsessed with stealing his daughter's cherry

in your dreams you have dived in the pacific, the atlantic, the adriatic sea

even the nile

and not one of them has enough strength or salt to wash the scent of him from off your skin

no razor blade cuts deep enough to polish his fingerprints from your glass surface

no floorboards will ever know your knees again

from now on, you will pray standing up

-mouth closed

prayer sometimes seems a little too close to rape

These Flowers were held by Broken Vases

prayer sometimes seems a little too forgiving

These Flowers were held by Broken Vases

after the storm

For two years my pulse sounded like a cemetery on life support

On Sundays I closed my eyes in church

Not because I was praying

-I did not want to see God

I was frozen in my anger

A glacier that desired to sink more than just ships

I needed alcohol

I needed empty bodies to lay with

Clouded glass houses that I could see through but get lost in

2 am showers cleansed me more than any baptismal pool ever could

For two years I paused my life just to replay the same heart aches

My sheets resembled ghosts ,not welcome home signs

I found my lungs tied to a tree

I had sown a mustard seed a while back

That's where I found my courage to breathe again

These Flowers were held by Broken Vases

God dug up my bones and found treasure when the rest of the world saw trash

BENEATH THE SOIL

This chapter is not for the bigot.

These Flowers were held by Broken Vases

are you too good and too much of a God to walk on the underground railroad with your jordans on?

These Flowers were held by Broken Vases

Black girl magic

raga brash rosa,

you walk as if all the muscle has lost its purpose within your rotator cuff,

shoulders slumped like the shadow of mothers holding their slain sons in streets

carrying no biases except, *the meat must be Black*

the magic has dripped dry from the curl of your crown

lips cracked/tongue swollen with vacillation

you act like you aint tired

you act like you'd be willing to give up your seat

young angela, your hips sit silent when you walk

there be no rhythm in your womanhood

These Flowers were held by Broken Vases

those girls laughed because you keep your knees bolt-locked against men posing as potential husbands

they wish their peaches held the juice and tightness of purity

has the activist in you manicured her nails?

no longer grasping things at the root?

pubescent woman, did you stumble the sista from your soul

from slavery to space shuttle

i couldn't help but call you,

clara even you couldn't see the queen in your brown

loretta/although you be lynching your truths

vonetta/ your flowers can bloom and bobsled through winter

this is to the young Black girl who forgot the mothers who gave birth to her

who forgot the village of nefertitis crooning for civil rights?

These Flowers were held by Broken Vases

i prayed for you in the hallway as you walked by

your name is beautiful

your name is more than just yours

These Flowers were held by Broken Vases

the color of baptisms and biases

in order for a black man to be a king and hold nobility as his prize,
he must wear his skin like hand-me down coats too small for angels to wear in winter
the oil ,
train-tracking itself through his veins must but hot enough to stain pavement and memories
he must be able to march up hills in the center of political hypocrisy and shine the lighthouse stored in his throat
freedom will ring like " i love you" notes from our ancestors
their blood spilled on clouds

in fields

 will forever be romance material
crucifixion material
in order for a man to lead boycotts, he must first allow the boy within his bones to grow out,

These Flowers were held by Broken Vases

to shave the uncertainty from his chin

learn to untie the knots from nooses in one hand and teach his sons to tie ties in the other

he must be able to see his dream and not allow his hands to hold it...

for a black man to be king and to drink at equality's well,

he must be thirsty

he must be tired...

These Flowers were held by Broken Vases

L pardoning mother's sins

the palms of priests could not paint the sacrifice i made when leaving,

i took some highs

and the lows i experienced did not come with spare tires,

in prayer i pleaded with God to pillow my breasts into being homes where you and your sister could lay your heads on

i waited years for him to *at least* whisper me an answer,

Jesus must have forwarded my calls and the third personality of the trinity played into the responsibility of its last name,

ghost

out of fear and pain i sandblasted motherhood from the pockets within my hands

drugs dressed as Love songs purred to me

These Flowers were held by Broken Vases

the title of mother was an evening gown too big to fit across my breasts

my hips were not woman enough to switch with the confidence of being a chef, doctor, and therapist all rolled into one

there was nothing super that proceeded this woman...

on many nights in strange rooms, i heard the walls ask to see proof that i was God's child and if my womb was worthy to have given birth to you

i had no intentions to voodoo my own children,

never asked to hoist the burden of being a drug addict and a mother

my womb never testified to being a renaissance man,

i can create masterpieces but do not have the capacity to Love them

i birthed seven dynasties and could not claim one /**not one**.

These Flowers were held by Broken Vases

∟ caffeine

if the best part of waking up is folgers in your cup

then why do you constantly try to change the taste of its coffee beans

i will not keep adding cream to my coffee

i repeat

i will not keep adding cream to my coffee

to the point where i can no longer recognize its original Black flavor

you will not keep stirring me up

just to fit the description of what's supposed to be in your cup

do not dilute who i am for what you want me to be

i am the coffee bean

These Flowers were held by Broken Vases

and without me, there's no coffee

so stop trying to change my pigment

as if my melanin is just a figment of your imagination

i am Black, i mean the coffee bean…

so please stop asking me to sacrifice my flavor to taste like your cream

These Flowers were held by Broken Vases

L mug shots of a broken heart

too many Black boys believe banging bricks and broads qualify them to break the sacrifice of their ancestors in half

divide freedom amongst themselves on street corners/place a price tag on time

tomorrow is too expensive to think about

dime bags pay by the hour but not for the hour

son, father time don't hand out refunds

these boys hands smell like cotton fields and disappear like gunpowder

lips chapped dry from talking about the same dreams that have been declared prisoners of war to fatherless homes

the hugs of overprotective mothers will not be your bunkers forever

These Flowers were held by Broken Vases

blossoming sons and bullets can break the heart and unhinge the hold from a mother's arms

career day in the hood resembles a game of flag football

an allegiance to either red or blue

they will crypt your dreams into stillness/smack the flavor of wanting more from your mouth

the american dream seems like an itch their fingernails and ambition will never be long enough to scratch

too many Black boys' legs look like fresh roses/learning to grow/hoping their thorns are seen as beautiful

these boys belong in outer space

they need to sing poems in outer space/ let the universe hear your voice planting seeds

they cannot bury you!

These Flowers were held by Broken Vases

don't ever let anyone tell you that Black boys didn't break bread with christ too!

Black boys have been rocking with christ before gold chains, they're just tired of carrying the cross

remember Golgotha

These Flowers were held by Broken Vases

ode to chicago boys

have you ever searched for your halo inside your silhouette?

told yourself that God replaced your angel wings with a snapback, jordans, and a street corner that had kodak captured too many of your childhood friends

these moments are not camera cute

but are acute to the truth

have you ever held your palms heavenward to see if all the crucifixions you have endured left any evidence

you're still making appointments for your resurrection

did you stumble sideways into egypt duffle bag boy, wondering if the sand would make a pharaoh out of you

didn't your fathers tell you that your penis nor your pride could petition pyramids

the sun and the moon will wayne on you lil boy

These Flowers were held by Broken Vases

no matter how much cash money you got

have you ever interrogated your birth certificate and asked if it belonged to someone else

some days you hold your breath, trying to abort the life from your lungs

you rock you pain polo fitted and burn bullets into your bodies like taboo birthmarks

i'm not judging you

i have also wondered if God voice mailed my prayers with no intention to check or consider them

stop looking to your shadow for advice

you have enough cornbread and Black eyed peas within your bones to make a million inmates march themselves to a second chance

–dream

These Flowers were held by Broken Vases

close your eyes without looking out the corners and pray to God

he will ambulance your heart away and stretcher your soul to safety

i have seen you stand in the rain, trying to taste what heaven is

you've been thirsting for so long...

stop looking for your shadow in these moments

observe that even God has ways of apologizing

...even God isn't too strong to cry

These Flowers were held by Broken Vases

shining serpent, thankful for God

did malcolm and martin drop to their knees when you approached heaven's gates?

Black body bearing more bullet holes than blood

damn blood, damn piru

they really made the gangsta inside of you lean six feet deep on a sidewalk of sin

snuffed the fire from your pen

and your palm

pulse no longer patriotic to the home of your body

where was your armor prince? makaveli you wrote *the art of war*

those wolves in sheep's clothing must've convinced you that your lyrics had enough tank and helmet in them to prevent you from being a chalk outline's wet dream

These Flowers were held by Broken Vases

they wanted to make sure you couldn't write or breathe

or have the right to breathe ever again

where fourth of july took place in the chest, pelvis, right hand and didn't stop until it said hello to your lung

maya must've hollered like a storm

mouth devoid of Poetry

only stanzas standing stock still

caged birds will always sing and sound like their sin

our sons will rise and be raised by streets if we don't Love them

pac, did you know your body would be a house robbed of its life?

so many people have

-waited

These Flowers were held by Broken Vases

-died

-needing answers from you

did brenda's baby ever grow up and out the trash like your roses in their concrete garden

who made you familiar with unconditional love

nina simone must've sang to this Black bird

cradled you to your grave as you watched the panther in you get swallowed by that jungle of a music industry

gangsta rap wrapped its savior in a body bag and shipped him home to his mother/did she see the shining serpent or a man thankful for God?

harlem has built many temples but you were a parrish where crooks could find forgiveness

did martin tell you he dreamed about you?

did malcolm say anything at all?

These Flowers were held by Broken Vases

did christ share his crucifixion story with you?

did muhammad surprise the doctrine in you as he stood clothed in majesty on the steps beside God?

on september 13, stanley lord was born

a ship captain that refused to help the passengers of the titanic

on september 13, tupac amaru shakur was murdered....

some people master the art of abandoning others, while others master the art of being abandoned...

These Flowers were held by Broken Vases

L before barack wore ties

i crawled into prayer

knees humble

hands meeting like Lovers after an argument

eyelids cemented tight like michelle embracing barack before Blacks were air force one fly/ bought air force ones by the dozen

my soles sold out

innocence consumed by a revolution

i am just now finding my genesis in this revelation

halfway to damascus

i cannot see my enemy next to me, let alone my own destiny

ray bans don't heal blind men

These Flowers were held by Broken Vases

but i will ray charles myself to the glory

i will lace up my sorrows from around my ankles

my body will not judas itself against my soul for soles that can't seem to see that i'm worth more than 23

i crawled into prayer because lately i've been feeling a lot like jonah…i've never been a good swimmer

especially in the stomach of whales

God, i've been drowning

i am trying to make my way from genesis to revelation but my legs gave out halfway,

circled in by a den of lions

God,

hold me close like michelle holds sasha and malia during ferguson septembers

father,

These Flowers were held by Broken Vases

you told me that you'd prepare me a table in the presence of mine enemies so that satan could tell me all about my problems while i kermit drink tea

my cup runneth over…

they don't know what i know… so i will david dance my way up the steps to your presence

unapologetically unconcerned with the weapons formed against me,

and on my darkest days,

i will keep psalms and proverbs in my palms until they join together into a promise…

collaboratively written with myles webster

These Flowers were held by Broken Vases

L home for you

i wish i could unbutton your middle name

throw it over your shoulders and make you wear the softness of it

did you know it means *lily*

you grew through more than just concrete

ever heard about the flower that erupted from the echoes of the earth or the cathedral that catapulted from within the sidewalk cracks of chicago?

i wish i could wash your feet with christ-like oil so they won't callous over when times get hard

-keep walking queen

- even if you drop your crown, allow your fingers to find strength to recover your birthright

there are too many broken girls hanging themselves on street corners, trying to find the savior within their sex

These Flowers were held by Broken Vases

young soldier girls, mirroring the hate their mothers have for their fathers

...some ghost just don't care enough to show themselves

do not become a trap queen

do not become trapped queen

do not be afraid to give birth to little boys who will boast about their mother, the superhero

do not be afraid to give birth to petals that will carry the scent of your fragrance once you are gone

...my wish is for your roots to find a place to call home

a place too comfortable to run from

These Flowers were held by Broken Vases

my mother's ghost is a white lady

white women have always seem to be the ghost of my mother

i guess she couldn't snuggle into someone who looked too much like her tragedy

maybe she tried to wash the sin and the soot from her skin

most of the women who have Loved the son in me, don't even look like me

yet, i am in their family portraits on thanksgiving

i am nailed to the mantle above the fireplaces in their hearts

these white women made me believe that i mattered

they made me see that color does not classify goodness

and having different pigments does not mean they cannot parent the pharaoh in me

thank you for loving the son in me

These Flowers were held by Broken Vases

thank you for loving the color and the cry in this Black boy

These Flowers were held by Broken Vases

the s on uncle tom's chest stands for slavery

aint nothing super about you man

you're a castrated hero

always talking about change but don't have seeds that will make revolutions grow

there is a hiccup in your chest, a stutter in your manhood, an excessive excuse that has romanticized your backbone

your ass can't even handle a sit-in

even your skin looks a little pale these days

campaigning for parties but ignoring poverty

aint nothing golden about you boy except that lie you bought from uncle tom

try and cash that check

put that tie,

These Flowers were held by Broken Vases

that camouflage figment of freedom and noose it around your neck

malcolm hated niggas like you

you have nothing to die for, you have distilled all the discipline from your blood

..didn't God teach you,

this skin can sing sacrifice like a canary on calvary

boy you're scared to be called radical. yet aint nothing polite about being a slave

shake loose yourself and get some harriet in your heels

...lead some slaves to freedom who didn't know they weren't free

you are a hand-me-down house negro

but this,

this right here is your eviction notice;choose the cotton fields or the railroads

These Flowers were held by Broken Vases

These Flowers were held by Broken Vases

└ Black girls & bandannas

girl,

you aint got to gangsta your heart and your guts against Love

told yourself to be,

too hard, **too** hood, **too** good to be got by some fool looking for a refill

after he just finished *feeling* and *filling* and dealing with someone's daughter

father fed your mother the same mess and you just aint eating off that plate

there's no need to even bring out the menu

sharing isn't always caring

or pairing up with these pigeons that can't match your fly

you're **too** eagle

too brown sugar and coconut oil for that

These Flowers were held by Broken Vases

penny pinching pieces of yourself together is worth more than the price they want to put on you

girl,

there is no such sin situated in softness when you have witnessed sojourners selling their truth

aint nothing nice about being sweet when sex says more than your mouth

girl,

you aint gotta be

or try to be

anything that you're not

God carved you from wood, not that fake shit they sale in the furniture stores

be beautiful

be your Black and smile like slavery aint ever touched your skin

These Flowers were held by Broken Vases

smile girl, your gangsta aint relevant if you never accept that first and foremost you're a queen

These Flowers were held by Broken Vases

∟ paprika

bullets/lightening creases through the cloud of Black flesh

scarlet

paprika garnishing *this* dish

hunger/ this place will leave your stomach stumbling/flailing to fumble its shoe-strings into sense

dusk slipping from eyes

the sun goes inside so quick lately

eyelids flutter into beautiful bluesy notes of dream

sidewalks crooning:

"scrub me clean"

a mantra moaned by the earth

soap/too gentle to scour sin

small white bubbles foaming,

These Flowers were held by Broken Vases

eyes of mothers foaming

their eyes the reflection of their sons hair

eyebrows

and those eyelashes that curled naturally

(he got them from her *too*)

sidewalks crooning:

kumbaya

why our sons/with their paprika blood

always flavoring these streets

always leaving their beds unmade,

making us believe they're coming back to sleep in their sheets

These Flowers were held by Broken Vases

L unapologetically trayvon

you can't calvin klein or michael kors your way into the east or west wing

they lynched men with more sensible style and politely tailored suits than your goons will ever have

are you too good to walk on the underground railroad with your jordans on ?

we pawned trayvon's 15 seconds of fame for sandra's pilot viewing

it wasn't as colorful due to the lack of skittles

but all the more colored

i asked God why he made me Black

me negro

me every bit the stepchild of being light skinned and off white

These Flowers were held by Broken Vases

why kemet gave birth to me

why did history catch a case of "forget your identity" but always wanted me to sale my fingerprints and then buy them back with bars

indicted my ethnicity

sentenced my race

i plead guilty your honor

i committed a crime in america

i walked down a sidewalk in lady liberty's cervix

discovered it had been raped by injustice

asked Jesus for strength

he was silent

they'd been hanging him before he was christ

he pointed to grace and mercy

These Flowers were held by Broken Vases

it was a Black man...my Black is unapologetic but was too much to be mentioned as the simon of the cyrene that i was....

These Flowers were held by Broken Vases

next time hold that boy's hand

before you shot him,

did you ask him if he'd ever been baptized?

did you know that boy aint ever been baptized?

next sunday, he promised his grandmother that he was going to be baptized

he told her he'd started walking by faith but you took that boy's sight

you kidnapped that boy's vision

ransomed it from his eyes

smothered his fight

do you know how hard his mother had to fight

to get him into college

fighting to keep her Black son alive

that boy's breath be scared to leave his body

These Flowers were held by Broken Vases

that boy's eyes be seeing everyone but God in the dark

they aint even killing us in the dark anymore

did you tell him that God's eyes be watching men like you dressing up as him,

with their guns in substitution for thunderbolts and communion robes that are law enforcement blue

did you tell that boy his body would be broken in two,

did you tell him that his body would be broken into

did you tell him that your grandfathers killed his grandfathers too?

please, did you at least give him time to ask God for forgiveness?

did you allow him to forget about hating you?

the last face he saw was yours, mr. officer,

did you give him the courtesy of holding his hand and telling him it was going to be alright even though it wasn't

These Flowers were held by Broken Vases

even if you were scared his flesh would skid-mark guilt upon you

before you claim things and people that are not yours

at least unfold their names over your tongue and swallow the universe of their being

consider their eyes,

consider the smile you jack hammered out their mouth

and for one moment, pray for the ones they received those parts from

These Flowers were held by Broken Vases

history lesson

on days where my feet seem to magnetize toward matters that disappoint my mother and i can't seem to avoid the cracks chiseled into the sidewalk

i ask God to help me discern between my shadow and my soul

to enfold the dauntless determination of accepting God is the divine director of this black imagery

i puzzle over why my history teacher never told me his grandfather wanted america to be spelled with three k's

i pledged my allegiance in a classroom that had no motive to make the man in the mirror appear to be a masterpiece and not just a master's piece

first day of class i heard teachers stutter over names that didn't taste white

i mean right

These Flowers were held by Broken Vases

made me proud that i had a real application friendly name/ "can't be biased toward me" type of name

framed by their ancestors just to be hung on the wall as something once touched by them

i never conscientiously consented to this fondling

of being a "well mannered"/ "you're so articulate" kinda *boy*

cloaked in confusion, i wore self-hate like it was stylish

all trends should not be followed

Black boys do not enjoy bearing bullets as their crosses

they'd rather bleed like johnnie mae chapell than to get on their knees

mama always said never let the floor have conversations with your knees

never allow hungry power men with red, white, and blue halos force you into believing God is a bigot

These Flowers were held by Broken Vases

on days where i fight for my white friends and family to understand me,

i ask God/is loving myself supposed to feel radical

These Flowers were held by Broken Vases

L sister

whenever someone mentions la

your name echoes excessively throughout my mind like belligerent bullets begging to make their point

i've been to los angeles once

but i don't think about all the angels lost there because you are the precipice of divinity gone rogue

a cleopatra that has denounced her throne

a crown that has been cracked open like an egg with nothing to birth forth but a generation of emptiness

your feet are tired of carrying around dead weight,

is this what the walking dead will look like, *you* ?

i have sweated out my dreams worrying about you

scalp scratched raw from the tick of terror i have become accustomed to

These Flowers were held by Broken Vases

bent

falling faithfully floor-ward

mouth opened reciting recipes of healing and deliverance to a God that can hurricane your soul loose

soul sister, where's your soul sister?

it hurts to see you prostitute the promise of life between your legs

it hurts to feel your tears land like burning sos signs in my palms

i can't save you

you have transformed yourself into a suicide letter having second thoughts

settling to live life only because the alternative isn't as clear

...don't betray the chicago streets that have copyrighted its fingerprints on the inside of your eyelids

you are still that girl fighting for her life,

These Flowers were held by Broken Vases

...mary fight the seven

...mary fight your hurt

God is in the kitchen, whipping up a batch full of healing

...mary won't you wait for the lord

if not for me,

...do it for the girl that died within you and left graffiti on the walls of your lungs

please, set your soul free

These Flowers were held by Broken Vases

epiphanies with nina simone

both hands gripped on the steering wheel

speakers on max, yet still not powerful enough to bring justice to the drumfire

the brass

the hurricane wind

the Blackness, the crown, the queen

of nina simone

45 miles per hour is just fast enough to lose yourself on this back road

and altogether *still* enough to cause belief that this hand-me down street is the physicality of your life

curved and confused

bending and winding and understanding to respect the unknowns and uncertainties of this journey

These Flowers were held by Broken Vases

...that's how trusting in God works, right ?

even if his answers are a balance between *"wait"* and silence

le ciel aide ceux qui s'aident

heaven helps those who help themselves

and patience is a virtue but what if i do not desire to be virtuous

what if i desire to free fall within the moment

popping at the seams

until i bleed with selfish intentions and happiness

they are more than mere abstractions

they can be touched and kissed and tasted with the tips of your fingers

the boise speakers bark like pit bulls fighting to conquer my eardrums

cautioning my soul, and nina simone summoning up a revolt within my bones- and the pit bulls holler

These Flowers were held by Broken Vases

when you feel really low

yeah, there's a great truth you should know

when you're young, gifted and Black

your soul's intact

i admit that i am a counterfeit superman addicted to kryptonite

there is a reliance in pain

a comfort that i am learning to unLove

as the song finishes…i think back to when i was 17, drunk and wet from falling in a pond

and i looked at my friend and whispered

"*God Loves you…*"

…i went and took my baptism by force

These Flowers were held by Broken Vases

soul like shakur

you got a soul that shakes the extra flour off the chicken

a golden glow that is manifested from being

battered

greased

fried

a voice that can transform a peep-hole perspective of the wilderness into being a promise land

unmake me

unstitch my disappointed soul

break me away from every slave and slave master that i have subjected the tapping of my feet to

dare not try to pop these broken fixtures back into place

there is an emancipation sitting cross-legged on the stoop of your tongue

These Flowers were held by Broken Vases

it has taught me to carry my water until it has been touched by God

aint no have, you possess a soul appropriated for incorrect speech yet remains a beautiful language

for aints

for gots

for slang

if that language were put into a song

it could speak the soul of angels

all those tired spirits with a common tune

there's no cuff on your lips

...let your essence flow

that batter

that grease

that fry

These Flowers were held by Broken Vases

but no death

no longer will your bondage sit on another's lips

rest restrained within another's tongue

you found the key to your chains'/ assata

realized that there was strength in being Black and woman

took your eyes off the ground

looked heavenward

 and saw a hand

battered

bruised

beaten worse than yours

grasped it

freedom never visited a man who never carried the weight of pain freedom came when you realized that slavery was a chain, a cuff on the mind that silenced lips and skinned souls bare

"but to become free, you have to be acutely aware of being a slave..." - assata shakur

Through

the concrete

These Flowers were held by Broken Vases

L supper from eden

saviors silently stilled away in syllables

we are the confessions of the creator

no lies

only light and Blackness can be found in our marrow

diamonds lining the interior of this-

-of our-

charcoal coated skin

gathering on a couch in jim crow's backyard,

protesting against the hunger in our hearts and in our stomachs

...a living room that has surrendered its identity for the sake of being an emergency room

These Flowers were held by Broken Vases

our organs; out and exposed

hearts heaving heavily to inhale the scent of a familiar soul and a timeless pain

...bits and crumbs of each other underneath our fingernails

have we been grabbing for one another in our prayers?

requesting a reaffirmation from God that loneliness can be shared

...that the weight of emptiness can be evenly carried

are we discovering the disinfectant for our scraped knees when we fell from grace?

a trinity trying to find its power and purpose

...even if it only lasts for one day

...for one fleeting night

within the molecules of this manifested moment

These Flowers were held by Broken Vases

maybe we found the gratitude of a soldier coming home from war,

the Love of an angel super gluing her wings back together

and the company of a traveler teasing her toes with new adventures

...this is our lives

...this is our moment

...this scenery matches sistine chapel ceilings

...standing on the shoulders of God

–oh, how high?!

for jerissa and jasmine

These Flowers were held by Broken Vases

jamillah

last night i saw an angel set aside her halo to pick up a guitar

her smile

brighter

than any iridium satellite frisbeeing itself across this universe

closed eyes,

lead to revolving doors that open to heaven

...paradise is so quiet when God and his angels are led to be speechless

with each strum,

sadness is broken down into small glittering diamonds

this stage is a jewelry store

golden be your guitar ballads

These Flowers were held by Broken Vases

last night i witnessed an angel waltz

with

sunlight

in the palm of her hands

hiccup Love notes that turned into fireworks

is *this* what happens when heaven has fourth of july

fireflies spilling from her stomach, dynamite glued under the

soles of converse

pine lake in november

champagne complimented with a side of childhood memories

let's talk about broke, let's talk about my lungs

knot

&

bent in my chest

you know me better than most people

i've always thought that you kept God's book of secrets hidden in your back pocket

...that you borrowed time's remedy for healing abused children

i've been running

running from God and from Love

but i found him on an early winter night tucked underneath november's arms

These Flowers were held by Broken Vases

wrapped in curly gray hair and pearls

"you can do anything that you put your mind to"

there has been a plea deal nailed to my chest

begging to be sentenced to a life less burdened than this one

communing over roasted chicken and fried cabbage i heard you say

"nothing worth having comes easy"

some places will always hold the magic that saved us from our childhood

these places will remind us why we can't quit

…we can't allow evil stepmothers to pick up our glass promises

…we can't stand still and wait for midnight to save us

we must learn to walk up to our crosses and submit ourselves to the pain in order to experience the freedom of resurrection

These Flowers were held by Broken Vases

⌊ semicolons are better than periods

morning comes,

you wipe away every trace of sleep and dream from your eyes

limp to the bathroom, not from morning drowsiness

−no one has ever taught you the importance of walking upright

or the sanctity in holding your head high

desperately you try to colgate and floss the self-destructive words from your mouth/ you make your gums bleed

the mirror has become a glossary of insecurities

rendering you insignificant: a suicide culture and the poster child for shattered things deeming themselves irreparable

unlovable

any lie that will land on good ground

inhale: boom

These Flowers were held by Broken Vases

exhale: boom

breathing should never feel or leave your soul resembling a vietnam battlefield

there are ears willing to cradle your burdens

eyes created to see the psalm 139:14 that is written all over you

don't dare stay dead, *defeated*

there is a lazarus napping in the hammocks of your marrow

death has a loose grip, an *"i declare thumb war"*-kind of hold on you

bankhead bounce your soul free

electric slide your way out of this inferno

whatever you do

lose control of your feet

These Flowers were held by Broken Vases

become a ii samuel and dance before the lord with all your

might

pick up your ephod

look toward the clouds

you see semicolons, not periods

suicide is a language; a descendant of braille

no noise

just feeling your way through

-you will survive

These Flowers were held by Broken Vases

Lloyd circle boy

i hope you still feel small standing beside the ocean

i hope you still bow your head when you talk to God at night

–never get too big for your britches

or rude enough to call your women bitches

you can't be walking around with that much dynamite in your mouth

always shoeshine your skin with that bottle of manners mama gave you from her childhood/ you can always find more in the medicine cabinet

some family heirlooms are forged from poverty and promises to get their children out of the house with the roaches

to save them from seeing the ghosts haunting the ghettos

i hope you still can taste the humble in the pie on thanksgiving

especially the tears cried and crushed into the cranberry sauce

These Flowers were held by Broken Vases

-dinners can be more work than wish

they don't know about the little boy from chicago

but i hope you will never forget him

i hope you will see the potential and the prayers pot-lucked into his smile

...i hope you still feel small standing beside the ocean

...i hope you never cut loose the "yes ma'am" and the "no sir" from the cliff of your uvula

when you lose humility, you become the sun without warmth/a flower without fragrance

These Flowers were held by Broken Vases

aa circle

my bed often feels like alcatraz

maybe parrys island on the not so bad days

either a concentration camp for my dreams

or

a war zone,

presenting me the opportunity to get up before the bullets hit my spine

before my achilles heel drops,

i discover i am a man dressed sometimes in God's shadow,

too slow and too tired to move with him

looking in the mirror compares close to seeing scripture in hebrew/ what do i become when i understand the translation

These Flowers were held by Broken Vases

i see the glory of God penciled in places of my soul without ever having reserved an appointment with my flesh

my name is william

jehovah is my smile's make-up artist

or *you* may know him or her as allah

he or she is too big to wear gender specific diadems

or sleep within the confines of a box labeled by days deemed appropriate to be spiritual

i am learning to Love and be Loved without asking my reflection if we deserve it,

if happiness has a guest list…

are we on it?

These Flowers were held by Broken Vases

hands,

those that belong to me and not the hands convincing me i belong to them

hands,

removed every land mine from within my chest

spring-cleaned the october skeletons hanging willie lynch style from around my voice

...my name is william

i have learned to Love myself,

beyond the faults of my parents' ill experienced fingers molding children to not be afraid of hugs

i am radiant

i am the goddamn sun

These Flowers were held by Broken Vases

i am bent, not broken

thank you,

all of you

who watched me burn...

my backbone is an 18 wheeler/swallows diesel

my feet kicks lightning from charcoal

These Flowers were held by Broken Vases

butterscotch

i heard dynamite clapping politely like gunfire within the undertones of your laughter

attesting to all the rainy days you've experienced hemmed underneath those beautiful eyelids

phantoms from your past pleated to the curvature of your smile

fingers fiddling to fix your life into a masterpiece

…breathing to break your broken interest into a basquiat triumph

there is a God that found you worthy enough to create

found you mozart enough to create a symphony out of your flaws

magma oozing from your majesty,

even your mistakes will create minerals, miracles

These Flowers were held by Broken Vases

crystals coming forth from your crevices...

fear is afraid that you will conquer it

that you will realize that there is a lynx lying dormant in your limbs

light humming like a nervous song singing from your ankles...

walk into your purpose

before you walked away

i kissed you

you said that you thought it was awkward

...maybe you aren't familiar with places that feel like home

past wishes

time has touched you in places i can only dream of knowing...

you are the first person that made me question if my hands were clean enough to hold someone's heart without staining it

your eyes are still bright; angel feather is your smile-soft and evidence of God's existence

your voice rings like heaven's doorbell

i could kiss your eyes, just to feel vision moving like broadway across my lips

today, i saw the chance i've always been too fearful to take

i do not trust myself to be enough

there is an uneasiness being bare,

to be removed from skin, secrets, and security

here, in this place

These Flowers were held by Broken Vases

we teeter on the tightrope between friendship and opportunity

we do not know if this glass is half empty or half full

we just know that our hearts make it refillable

we teeter like lifeguards on the sideline

wanting to see if this *"thing"* we have going on will ever float

but it was great seeing you today

i smiled like it was my birthday

and i could've kissed you like this place was christmas and this table was the mistletoe

when i prayed over my chicken florentine crepe

i asked God if he would allow you to see yourself like *i do*

you are a picasso

this world is the gallery fortunate enough to showcase you

you are one in a million

These Flowers were held by Broken Vases

moonshine makes mondays wash down a little easier

it rinses the taste of risk from your mouth

...one day, i may take a chance on you

or one day we will meet up again

faces showing tracing of some of the places we have been

i will listen to you speak about your family and your music

and i will think...

"do you still write songs about me?"

"what would it have been like if it were me?"

These Flowers were held by Broken Vases

L *untitled*

a broken heart can cause you to discover more treasure than any pirate ship

fileted aortas and diced up ventricles can become the candy trail leading you to who you really are

nighttime is more than bedtime stories and fairytales

you must coach your heart into sleeping in the same rooms you made memories in

God has not given us fear

but enough faith to resurrect rusted buildings and straighten the spine of the leaning tower of pisa

broken hearts have more prayers vested into their pockets than altar calls with deposit slips

These Flowers were held by Broken Vases

shattered organs strung along like violins at orchestras can teach you a lesson on repeat until you press play on happiness

cracks in your heart is God adding graffiti to your soul

i have bled dry like the red sea parting for staffs soaked in sun rays

like sunrooms in heaven

...only God can furnish you with healing

...houses only become homes when God is present

These Flowers were held by Broken Vases

sneaking onto rooftops

we will climb ladders higher than any fire escape will allow

searching for the right spot on the world's rooftop/the hearth of heaven's heart

a secret place where we can write letters beginning with

"i have forgiven you"

addressed to people that disappear after breaking hearts

in this refuge, it rains just to make the tears on your face feel more at home

bourbon is always served alongside a humming radio

lauryn hill *to zion* is on repeat

in this place, stretch your arms and believe you can fly/because **you can**

moments like these kiss your neck, letting everyone know it has touched you

These Flowers were held by Broken Vases

it will take the place of your favorite sunday meal and when you taste it,

your mouth will be left longing for more.

peace is a rare dish.

shaky knees

sex has always been my apology letter to the people i wanted to Love but didn't know how to

my fingers always managed to fumble their hearts right after touching down in their beds

how many one night stands can one person receive without making statements to the tune of:

"we can't keep doing this."

one day,

i look forward to praying to God about you

free styling about free falling forever,

fingers feeling for more than just a quick hit

playing knock knock run on hearts has gotten old

i crave conversations that create climaxes in my mind and orgasms in my soul

These Flowers were held by Broken Vases

my heart will tremble, shaky knees for you

i haven't met you yet

but i have reserved a spot for you in my heart

excuse the clutter, i had some guests who stayed a little too long

but it's all i can give

sex used to be the way i Loved

found my name hibernating underneath their heavy breathing and i thought i was important enough to stay there

now, i just write poems, hoping they'll find it worth reading one day...

maybe then i'll be able to write about the sunrises and the butterflies that occasionally take flight in my stomach

L promise land

These Flowers were held by Broken Vases

your heart: a frantic symphony

a sea of galilee progeny

storms of your degree exists with the desire of needing to be calmed and claimed as someone's blessing

anticipating footsteps that will travel the expanse of your heart

-not to damage nor to pollute

but to be a symbol of reassurance that someone has faith enough to acknowledge it

to fall all the way in

even when they lose sight of saving grace

no matter the magnitude of pharisees that will challenge them

they will appear as their own witness

-their testimony will be valid

-their Love will be vivid

These Flowers were held by Broken Vases

a rainbow of hues: patience, kindness, contentment, humbleness

there is someone who has seen the river of egypt that is your head

the euphrates that is your feet

you are a promise land

someone is wandering the wilderness

hoping…bent-knee, eyes window shutter tight

praying to inhabit you

"the priceless gift of life is Love, with the help of God above."

יקר מפז מתנת חיים היא אהבה, עם העזרה של האלוהים

These Flowers were held by Broken Vases

heart is not a synonym for floor mat

-for you

These Flowers were held by Broken Vases

∟ goodbye

i always get a lump the size of the sun in my throat when it's

time for goodbyes

the word sizzles out and stains my hands, my feet, and my

hope with sunspots

ask me how it feels to carry around empty envelopes from the

past,

hoping they will one day become invitations from the future

ask me how it feels to surrender entire relationships to the

embassy of a two syllable entity:

These Flowers were held by Broken Vases

goodbye

how can one word holocaust my heart

...hopefully i will learn to undress my expectations

parole my promises

-i will learn how to do this goodbye thing

-be as strong as a tree in the fall

-let leaves unhook themselves from me until spring...goodbye

These Flowers were held by Broken Vases

God did not create you to be an apology letter to anyone

–for you

These Flowers were held by Broken Vases

cognac man

before we meet up again

i have a confession that has cemented itself to the sides of my throat

please forgive this quicksand heart of mine; it swallows whatever and whoever uses it for finding their footing

...give me a second to dust the limp and lackluster "*i Love you*" that has lingered far too long from off my lips

well, here it goes

last week when we were folded into each other's bodies like two stars expecting to explode into one giant galaxy,

i silently set up surveillance around the perimeter of your soul

wired your heart

monitored the nervousness in your palms

you sweat your secrets like diaries in a fire

These Flowers were held by Broken Vases

-i found fresh fingerprints footnoted in your mind

-a voice that wasn't mine but sounded sure it was in the right place

-a shadow standing straight and confident in the doorway of your arteries

is this who keeps your heart beating?

is this why i can only see you at night?

are you afraid i will see him on the skyline of your eyes in the daytime?

Anxious your self-possession will melt away and i will see your eyes lined with dreams of you and *him*

before we meet again i need you to know

i saw a pair of men's shoes too big to be mine underneath our bed when i was vacuuming

and a new light in your eyes and i apologize for not having time to change the bulb

These Flowers were held by Broken Vases

but,

i wanted you to know…

i noticed the crown royal in the fridge

…baby, i've always been a cognac man

These Flowers were held by Broken Vases

L honest.

i still have nightmares

my mother is often the monster hiding in the closet

i have a hard time loving people/they either lie to me, themselves, or God

some days my loafers are heavy with the lead of combat shoes,

my heart is purple and this soil smells of afghanistan after suicide vests being detonated

i have childhood trauma but God is teaching my hands to search for band aids in the dark

there is an understanding that raising blankets over my head will not hide the light of my halo,

These Flowers were held by Broken Vases

and if my heart is to be broke by *you*

God told me where he keeps his extra tube of superglue and second chances

These Flowers were held by Broken Vases

L dancing for God in the rain

have you ever danced for God in the rain ?

your heels held hostage to an untamed praise hitting the water

trusting that in this storm he will not only keep you but increase you

have you

have you ever stripped down to your humble parts

held a hallelujah within your heart so big even heaven couldn't hold it and deaf ears couldn't help but hear it

have you ever praised God inside a hurricane

without thought or reservation resting in the hopes for the sun to set you free

you must learn to be content

These Flowers were held by Broken Vases

no matter what mountain may mistake its size as too big for God to move

to what extent have you settled your soul to see

to experience something glorious

something hard but honest

you are bent, not broken

his hand is the breeze

this rain,

the tenacious testament of his Love,

an ocean that laughs at limits

but there is no drowning here, only saving grace

have you ever danced for God in the rain

worshipped without restraint

wild

i know the sun hasn't been out in a while

These Flowers were held by Broken Vases

but this season is a high school type of temporary

God is the assurance of hope

come, won't you dance for him?

These Flowers were held by Broken Vases

L second chances

i almost went back

parallel parked my purpose in my comfort zone and got out

time had really gotten hold of me

...i always felt the weight of wishing for a new minute

how about just giving me a second...

bottles became biblical

i was a disciple dining with death and destined for destruction

i opened them daily,

broke bread with my hurt and refused to speak to God

i almost went back

helplessly hit rewind

These Flowers were held by Broken Vases

descended into a familiar state of depression and renamed it *"i'm ok"*

suicide sanded herself down so she wouldn't appear to be a bad option and placed a priceless bid on my life

i almost signed the check...

recycled reasons to give up and reused them every chance i got

tears couldn't translate what my heart felt

i was a man that didn't have the resources to prove it

no words could compensate for the heavy emptiness that occupied my soul... i almost went back to my old skin

temporarily thought about trying on my uncomfortable 16 year old smile

stepping into a soul seduced by sadness

i realized that i controlled the expiration date on my happiness

...life gets hard

These Flowers were held by Broken Vases

...but it's worth living

These Flowers were held by Broken Vases

⌊ tomorrow wants your smile

it stormed last night

raindrops the color of calvary

leaving behind the scent of farewell and suicide letters

yellow was the only color in the rainbow with enough courage to shine today

a souvenir from God, reminding you of the pieces of sun doing pirouettes inside your chest

–a one legged battle cry to breathe

...breathe

you will not become another tragedy within the fields of ketchum, idaho

life is not one big game of musical chairs

These Flowers were held by Broken Vases

you are too strong to quit even after the music stops…eyelids closed, palm to chest

feel that music

touch and believe in that second chance going at the speed of 60 to 100 beats per minute

it rained last night and God cried so hard

heaven felt him scrape his knees

the earth shook

&

broke

and healed

yesterday, 86 of his children forgot they were good enough

they could not see the hand-wave of tomorrow, their ears were in Love with all apologies and fighting temptations to the tune of paul williams…

it rained last night

yellow was the only color in the rainbow with enough courage to shine today

...life is worth living; if you're looking for a sign not to kill yourself

this is it...

death is a pill that burns the lining of your throat on its way down

renders you speechless

makes a mockery of your plans for tomorrow and only bows its head to God

These Flowers were held by Broken Vases

unashamed

she caught us in the hallway

both our lips and anything we held as ours became hers

she was added to this equation intended for two

i did not care

my heart wasn't affluent in being clothed

nakedness has always been my inheritance

bearing all of myself in my hands

this secret was my cross and everything about you was golgotha

and although her eyes were on us

my eyes could not have been removed from yours

in that hallway,

sunday came early and you were my unrepenting testimony

you will forever be that battle scar i wear proudly when my grandkids ask

" *granddad, who taught you to be so free?*"

"*where did you get all that healing from?*"

...she caught us

hearts unzipped, and our modesty around our knees

we must've resembled a museum for wild things that had grown weary of accommodating everyone's hearts but their own

in this wilderness i found the God who knows my name-i found the whisper of his promise on your lips

even when i force friday night to change her name into a saturday morning

i want you to know that your fingertips never have to make an appointment with me

These Flowers were held by Broken Vases

even if it is only so that you can remember what your own pulse feels like

These Flowers were held by Broken Vases

carpet confessions with domonique

i have felt the holy ghost send out emancipation from my ankles

a dancing off of shackles

a praise earth-quaking itself through my palms

a tug tug behind my umbilical cord

i don't always have the courage to wear freedom

but when i do, i wear it well

i cLove-hitch it around my throat

truth is my only diction

i have broken myself in the bed of others

passed around my water, placed my heart on silver platters and served it with well intentions

only God can recycle your bitterness

These Flowers were held by Broken Vases

wipe it down, blow the soot off and rename it into a testimony

i have watched myself die a thousand deaths

placed myself into hands that i knew couldn't Love me

and i stayed

not out of Love

but pain has always been flirty and familiar

...but God has always been faithful

he has always cpr'd me back to life

called me beLoved when i believed myself to be bare of beauty

i have felt the holy ghost invite itself into my feet

this is a dance dripping with redemption

a worship that only the broken and the forgiven can interpret

despite my flaws

i am here, wrapped in redemption and hallelujahs parading on this salvaged property

These Flowers were held by Broken Vases

my God, i could have been dead

pathetically pleated against the walls of a coffin six feet under

the lord knows i have swam through numerous storms

...but he placed me in a boat

threw me a paddle and told me *"you won't drown, but you must learn to row"*

These Flowers were held by Broken Vases

I aint ever

saving my sex and myself for my wife

loving only God because these people will kiss your voice straight from your throat and use all the Love you ever had as a chaser

commit to a relationship? no, not me

i don't know how to Love

never knew how to crease my arms into a hug

to hold a person and let them know that *it's going to be ok*, even if i didn't believe it to be true

...i only looked forward to going to sleep,

never to be awake

i aint ever being sober again

These Flowers were held by Broken Vases

i'm going to find all the lessons my father forgot to teach me and find my doctrine between the legs of the people that confuse sex with something serious and acquaint it with Love

i haven't prayed in a while, told myself that God stopped listening

that's old news, that old tune you drink and listen to the blues to

history that gets picked up by my voicemail

aint got time for

this

that

or none of that fluff they've been selling me

i aint stupid

God aint deaf

my pain was only trying to warm up the seat for my purpose

These Flowers were held by Broken Vases

the truth is my gospel and i'm learning to testify my way to freedom

it's never easy talking about the parts of yourself that you don't like

...we all have cellulite connected to our souls

it's not easy to face the monsters that play with the skeletons in our closets

-but it's necessary

These Flowers were held by Broken Vases

finding God

aint no altar ever truly introduced me to God

no handshake balanced with the harmonies of a hymn set my mind free

no book,

no holy conversation translated into ink taught me to Love without condition

the hands of my heart struggled against steeples

against church pews

against pulpits

my ankles trembled at the thought of a religion that demanded more money from me than a tenth of my time

they always seem to manipulate malachi

hands up

These Flowers were held by Broken Vases

eyes closed

his Love

his favor

his mercy transcends

all these rubix cube addictions

my eyelashes have only caught the light of his sovereignty

my knees only got me closer to whatever floor i was kneeling on

it was my heart

it was from every hum of my organs that i recognized God in the sun

God in the son

so, excuse me please

i found God in ways not taught…

These Flowers were held by Broken Vases

stop asking people to give you your voice

-for you

These Flowers were held by Broken Vases

i am willing

your smile---

the sun which accommodates my ripening core

there is no need for roots

i am willing to be ungrounded for you

purely uprooted and reckless

shaken loose from every crevice of foundation

content with theoretical Love

knowing there is no law

nor a dissertation molded into words that could explain the life

i feel for you

this breath

These Flowers were held by Broken Vases

rejoices in my lungs because i know that our heartbeats can collaborate on dance floors, even when there is no sound

our smiles are music enough

our palms, clattering with nervousness are destined to caress flowers back to life after being familiar with thieves whose only desire is to bottle the scent of their perfume

These Flowers were held by Broken Vases

L naked

strip

present me the raw beauty of your nakedness

our hands have been longing to undress one another's insecurities

wanting to exist within the golden sand of cleopatra and marc antony

embracing the boldness of *"this is me"*

and having the strength to say , *"..and i will accept every flaw that God has chiseled into you"*

strip

dismantle your walls so beautifully

kodak wishes it could capture your exotic esteem

These Flowers were held by Broken Vases

present yourself as the artwork that the master created in genesis

no gallery is worth your truth

even i question if my hands are glass enough to care for you roses

i will peel away all of me

offer it to you

unfiltered

untouched as this

and you will see my bruises

...your ears will behold the orchestra of my soul

These Flowers were held by Broken Vases

L these flowers were held by broken vases

these flowers were held by broken vases

the stepchildren of hands that melt against the harshness of the world

cradled by hearts woven from linen,

strong enough to staunch the bleeding from old wounds but were not intended to survive snowstorms

secured by promises that were engineered to be compliant with technical difficulties

these flowers

comforted by mouths that dare not be seen holding hands with the truth in public

these flowers

though dropped and wounded by shattered glass remain crucifixion beautiful

These Flowers were held by Broken Vases

this type of strength can only be attained through suffering

&

surviving

pain changes the best parts of people

these flowers

were held by people that attempted to place a price-tag on the royalty engrained within your purpose

you cannot wager with God about your worth

these flowers

were dominated by fingers unsure of their ability to hold anything except their own ego

...watered by insults

fertilized with the most potent of hopes to be held by hands that were strong enough to embrace their own vulnerabilities before ever trying to rescue anyone else from their own

vases break

These Flowers were held by Broken Vases

even the ones crafted to be indestructible

people break, even the ones we need to be strong for us

these flowers

will remain beautiful, even after their petals have become intimate with the ground

our garden was uprooted and placed in hands that could not withstand the heat within our petals

nor feel the light of God living within our bones

these flowers wither

(but always return in the spring)

These Flowers were held by Broken Vases

L breadcrumbs leading to the cross

i didn't trust my heart to Love you enough

unsure if my hands could push pass the weight of my sin and rise in worship

...any excuse would do

dutifully i denied the call of the holy ghost

pitifully positioned my palms over my ears to block out God's voice

there was an obligation to my incarceration

an indignant interest to remain in shackles and in bondage to my addictions that temporarily teased me with their fraudulent appearances of peace

i was a wavering house

a building requiring renovation from God

These Flowers were held by Broken Vases

a broken heart that needed more than just a band aide but spiritual healing

i heard a knock on the door one day

and you came in and communed with me

effectively executed open heart surgery on my soul

i was a sampson and david all rolled into one

attempting to assassinate my multitude of goliaths while entertaining delilahs

yet i desired God

even when i didn't know psalms 37:4, i became the manifestation of it

i found peace petitioning me

God's Love leading me

failures falling underneath my feet

providing themselves as stepping stones

These Flowers were held by Broken Vases

...undoubtedly, i will fall

stumble alongside sin

struggle to stand with my scraped-knees

but

i will remember the cross still has power

and it is faith that blesses hymnals to heal

These Flowers were held by Broken Vases

canadian skies, chicago soul

there would be a curtain of butterflies with guilt tied to their wings

hanging in my stomach if i apologized for this addiction

when i was younger, a boy whose eyes only saw in dream-vision because reality was a shade too dark to live brightly in

i prayed...

i prayed for God to staple wings to my shoulders

it took me years to learn to fly, but oh God

dear gracious God

i found my wings folded into my spine

...sometimes i wonder if i wear the hallelujah well enough around my ankles

These Flowers were held by Broken Vases

because without God's grace i would have tripped

i would have stumbled between the cracks in the sidewalks of chicago and signed over my birthright to a street corner

there are days when the air in my lungs feel like plutonium

and that's okay

even sunflowers become unsure of God's presence when the sun aint anywhere to be found

they bow their halos in prayer, searching for a reason to lift their crowns in darkness

God presented me a canadian skyline just in case the lamp on the nightstand wasn't enough to light up this moment

every day i learn to walk again, allowing my knees to bend in this two-step Love affair with life

today,

i will wear my skin like the most beautiful piece of canvas stretched across bone

These Flowers were held by Broken Vases

this smile will cripple tears

this laugh will wage war on anything that opposes freedom

i could never

i would never repent for this addiction

these endless one-night- stands with airplanes, Poetry in afghanistan, vegan restaurants, house music in the hollywood hills, and running through fields in foreign countries

being broken bore my signature better than any contract could

i'm finding the treasure in happiness

and dear God,i found you

-you never left

These Flowers were held by Broken Vases

cab rides to heaven

i promise to tell all your jokes to God...

when i die, i will sneak out the back door and leave the coordinates to paradise so that you can mail me my favorite bottle of white wine

do you think i can hitch a ride to heaven that late at night?

do you think God will leave the porch light on for me?

pinky swear to tell your friends about me

tell them the truth

tell them about the Black boy who was not afraid to burn down the bitterness he was born into

sing the songs about my sin and about the crooked confidence within my smile

jigsaw my life into a beautiful but honest obituary

These Flowers were held by Broken Vases

i promise to tell kat that you're smiling a lot more these days

and that you're learning to Love without having the training wheels screwed on so tightly

...don't take my passing too hard

i went away easy with the lord

quietly solicited my soul and sorrow away from my body

do you think the taxi will know the address to heaven?

do you think a sinner like me will find the spare key to the pearly gates or will i be too short to ring the doorbell?

i wonder if my melanin will appear miraculous instead of mud-like and moody

...i promise to tell God that you told me to tell him to take good care of me

...i promise i will wait

legs, indian-style folded with patience

These Flowers were held by Broken Vases

…and just in case the taxi doesn't run that late at two in the morning

i will rent elijah's chariot and rescue your risks into the safety of my backseat

i will excommunicate sound from my ears until i hear you say my name

but please, until then…

don't forget me

These Flowers were held by Broken Vases

L first encounters with Love

if i had to describe your smile

i would fish-hook the thesaurus out of God's throat

thumb through its pages until i found the synonym for sun

&

write you down as the only candle in a world full of darkness

i would sleep in your flowerbed until our roots tangled into a testimony of time and timber

-kiss the genesis of your neck until you feel a revelation pull your toes into a curl

i just want to...

drive at 100 miles per hour

with my eyes closed with you

These Flowers were held by Broken Vases

&

trust God to take the wheel

this Love is cpr certified

there is an unparalleled beauty enclosed in the creases of your lips

an impolite truth that licks the salt off the rim

...you are a walking shot glass

and you will always be my poison of choice

you will always be enough to eradicate the meaning of sobriety...

These Flowers were held by Broken Vases

I queen

you, queen

was the poem that i always wanted to recite

to read between the lines of your passion

conscientiously creating conclusions that your queendom had been broken into on too many occasions

...too many jokers had presented themselves as kings before your feet

causing you to question the quality of your crown

you, queen

are everything that eve imagined herself to be

...my chest will be an altar for your dreams at night

These Flowers were held by Broken Vases

...my palms will tissue the tears from your almond eyes

even if i have caused them

...you are a walking stanza

dancing cursive

beautifully written

but hard to understand

These Flowers were held by Broken Vases

L the son is shining

in the darkest of places

you serve as the light of the world

the son, that needs no permission to shine

strip the king of kings naked

yet you are still clothed in majesty

loving not only them, but me

unborn,

yet you allowed your body to be the altar for my transgressions

lord, we were all hostages to sin

yet you paid the ransom

bankrupt in our spirit, foreclosed in our minds

These Flowers were held by Broken Vases

no grave could have ever buried your sacrifice

no tomb could ever commemorate the blood that you shed for me

on calvary

spat on

beaten

they tried to lynch the spirit right up out of you

hell could not prevail

all out of Love

and this is my hope…

you rose

when fridays come, you have presented me an inheritance of sundays to rise

you rose

These Flowers were held by Broken Vases

conquering all of time

the son, who needs no permission to shine

These Flowers were held by Broken Vases

L under the influence pt. 1

drove drunk and dizzyingly dangerous down a dark road

deliberate within my indecision to stay...

unsure if commitment was a comfortable place furnished with a couch that could pillow my pain and complimentary massages for this sore back

spun around into a u-turn, shoe sole sitting sinfully heavy on the gas pedal

heart weighed down by the guilt

you are the only turn worth getting

pulled over

These Flowers were held by Broken Vases

ticketed

placed into the backseat of a cop car

for

these wrists have pled guilty to being wishbones found wriggling on the clearance rack,

only being able to live up to granting certain wishes...nothing requiring too much magic

but they are willing to be accessorized with handcuffs and call them watches for you

time will emancipate the loneliness alcatrazed to our hearts

my heart would stutter during a breathalyzer, stumble like marbles across straight lines when asked about *you*.

i drove halfway to my destination,

brain bursting past the barriers of ego and self-righteousness

tired of this old garment of sedated thinking

These Flowers were held by Broken Vases

realizing that my reason for smiling

my vacation on rainy days was fifty miles behind me...

will you open the door when my knuckles demand to come in

will you find the courage to find the spare *second chance* hidden in your sock drawer and hand it to me without anger or shame

if i ask to hold you like breath in lungs,

could you surrender?

could you scoot over and make room for me?

These Flowers were held by Broken Vases

L under the influence pt. 2

even my ears recognize how your knuckles feel on my door

somethings aren't meant to make sense

it is a sound of being all too accustomed with facing bolt-locked doors and fearing if they will remain that way

but i am yours for the asking,

so my legs will always lift like "*i Love you*" notes folded into paper airplanes and greet you at any entrance

there has been food in the oven ever since you left, but i'm not sure if it's warm enough to soothe your hunger pains

before boldness bends my fingers into bringing the door open,

i wipe every trace of tear from my eyes

smooth the wrinkles from my shirt and position my palms to become pedestals to lay your apologies on

These Flowers were held by Broken Vases

you: i'm sorry

me: i'm sorry that i didn't fight for you to stay

pride has no place here.

you: ....umm, you smell good.

me: i took a shower. i waited up for you just in case...

throat tight, this is what it feels like to be clothed yet vulnerable...

you: is there room in your bed for me?

there is food in the oven, waiting to meet your hunger,

me: always.

let's Love and litter this world with our footprints

let's Love like tomorrow will not wait...

These Flowers were held by Broken Vases

just because it feels good, doesn't mean it belongs to you

-for you

These Flowers were held by Broken Vases

L heaven in you

faucet heads fixed above us like halos

shower scenes scaffolding mighty close to what heaven must've looked like in the eyes of adam and eve

ribs mighty close

lips mighty moist

hands mighty desperate to grasp hold of something that feels not familiar

but right

melting millennials making room for their hearts' sake or opening doors casually

heartbreak has become something normal

 an expected malady

These Flowers were held by Broken Vases

…Poetry, showers, and a need to feel wanted are all ingredients a recipe crafted from God's romance novel

we just want to make it to his bookshelf

…this is what it must feel like to bathe in angel falls,

niagara can't even fathom this truth, this earth quaking romance of rigid strength

…shower heads heal hearts having too many pieces missing from them,

these kisses promise to linger long after our bones bend and break …but will these hearts hiccup into forgiveness if not handled carefully…

These Flowers were held by Broken Vases

loving them was the storm, loving yourself is the paradise

-for you

snapshots of angels

...what makes you mortgage your heart out to me?

the credit of my fingers have been known to disrupt the assurance of spines

do you trust me enough to blow the dust from off the shelves of your heart?

i'm no good with my hands but my lips can teach you a thing or two about dreams and flying

these eyes can teach you a thing or two about capturing snapshots of angels...

...are there really nights carved from God's promises made vacant for us to have our Love affairs in?

These Flowers were held by Broken Vases

∟ easy street divulgences

after twenty-three years,

my shadow still sneaks up on me and i have no idea which sidewalk i should allow it to find a home on

my feet have been locked into too many designer shoes designed to keep me right where i'm standing

-damn, they're right

i am a mannequin

all this time i thought they've been paying me compliments

there is a juggle in my wrists and no one seems to notice or care about the gamble in my limp

i walk like dice/begging God to find some luck along the way

even if he turns out to be a wizard that can't give me the courage to Love myself

on some days,

These Flowers were held by Broken Vases

particularly on sundays when God seems a little too quiet,

my mirror mix-matches its identity and becomes a pseudonym/ a billboard to broadcast my insecurities

being honest is always easy-bake conventional until you have to produce something real about yourself

let's talk about what happens when you don't have enough stamina or enough endurance to Love yourself past your regrets

dear fear,

on too many occasions i found myself lame,

a cripple and a conduit for your games

you voodooed my bones

i couldn't see the magic in my own smile anymore

the mirror provided a glare against God's approval

dear fear,

These Flowers were held by Broken Vases

i am learning to wear my name like it was tailored to fit my shoulders...

i am learning to rub my bones together until i am on fire without fear of failing

...i will not be afraid to Love the person in the mirror

even when there are some streaks too stubborn to wipe off

netflix & chill

the first time i hugged you, it felt like a warm shower after three days of being in a grave of heartache

who knew that embraces could resurrect you back on the pilgrimage to your purpose

your palms ice creamed and netflixed my afflictions

you were the best break up remedy

everyday i binged-watched your smile

held your name tightly as i drifted into sleep

thank you,

for signing your name between my ribs and having the courage to Love me like it was your responsibility...

These Flowers were held by Broken Vases

These Flowers were held by Broken Vases

L apology

this is an apology letter,

my proclamation emancipating all the hearts that still labor on the plantations of my heart

there was never any freedom found in loving me

i never meant to lead you on,

completely oblivious to the "follow the leader" sign hot glue gunned to my back

...my words back then never had that much backbone

i couldn't even lead myself,

my feet were still unwinding from underneath my mother's lips

i Loved like plot-holes at funerals

These Flowers were held by Broken Vases

filling myself up on dead things

my skin was a cemetery within itself

so many people buried their soul and their secrets on its surface

individuals placing initials on my body with their tongues

did they not know saliva can't leave so much as a stain on souls...i'm sorry for all the nights i made you question your worth?

and your birth

...self, i'm sorry that i couldn't rescue you sooner

but i want you to know,

you are more than worth saving

more than silver

more than gold

These Flowers were held by Broken Vases

L unrequited Love

never find rest on churning seas that challenge the unwavering Love you have for life

God will always remain the calming eye of any storm threatening to conquer your unconquerable soul

there is a strong tower grounded within the palms of his presence

tranquility tempered into the steel of his voice

there is a testimony waiting, open handed to embrace you on the other side of every pursuit in which you undertake

brilliance bruised like acrylic birthmarks on every inch of your canvas

yes, you have tarried on mountaintops with your wings nestled close to your sides

These Flowers were held by Broken Vases

but there is a flight,

a freedom waiting for you to coast on the tempest of change

happiness is a fleeting accessory that too many souls wear without procuring the garment of peace

stitched from a cloth lacking passion which results in a destruction worse than death

a fabric flannelled from synthetic fibers

family, friendship, and faith in God is a tartan calico that will keep you warm on winter nights

no matter how dark it may appear, if you reach out far enough

you will discover the horizon hiding fetal position in God's hands waiting to guide you

there is a unique incandescence ascribed to the most high's presence

run for him, like the deer pants for streams of water

These Flowers were held by Broken Vases

allocate your soul to a desperation that is destitute of malicious intent

in times where finish lines appear more fable than friend,

rejoice in the personification of joy

devote your smile to being an entreaty for captivating broken hearts and foot soles too tired to keep going

tell them about the God that picked up your petals and painted the colors from Black to beautiful

death has no power here

for this is a marriage of surrender and pure affection

arrogance is an emperor that thrives on conquests consisting of congregating with fools involving themselves with conversations thirsting acumen

God's grace is a generous bank knowing no deficit

able to abolish the limitations of financial fences

These Flowers were held by Broken Vases

gracious in forgiving loans loaned out to sinners that will forever be unable to repay the lender

his mercy dwells in a court of righteous justice and pacific predication

hasty hugs have rendered many with broken ribs, lungs lifting legacies of dysfunction with every breath they take

learn to Love even when you juggle the fates of unappreciation and the betrayal of brotherhood

time and patience will be a brother in your old age

nothing is promised

take advantage of the bliss God bequeaths the blessed with

never allow your passion to be jailed

nor domesticated

following your purpose is a powerful wave that must constantly wash upon the seashores of your soul

These Flowers were held by Broken Vases

today will always be a reminder why we can only get brighter

tupac wasn't afraid to be a misfit

nor was dali

nor should you

find the rainbow dwelling within the depths of your shaky knees and bambi-like footing

God is humming a song to fix every fault that karma may have missed

his vengeance is fair

but his Love is too large to be embodied by one

transcend the limbs and the muscle of your ego

Love like a forest fire trying to find the right place to lay its head

do not be inconsiderate

These Flowers were held by Broken Vases

this is the true essence of being successful,

sure of God's promises...

wear your scars like ancient unalome

tattoos of sacred averment that God is always with you

...even when we rather settle for seeing our seasons as orphanages than hospitals for growing pains

you

we

us

must be stouthearted

fearless saints

undaunted rebels against the hardships of life...

These Flowers were held by Broken Vases

road trips to heaven courtesy of my living room

testimonies waving in this room,

white flags...

we are making peace with our hurt

surrendering secrets without shame,

this is our sin on a cross built with our hands

washing the behind our ears and scrubbing the poor paint job from off the surface of our chests,

you cannot pretend your broken parts whole

cemeteries have been laid here

skin molded into concrete

we have harbored hurt like ships with un-deployed sails

stifled in silence

we are here to worship

These Flowers were held by Broken Vases

regurgitating broken glass

it's painful to heal, skin stretching over bone again

God will blow the dust from your lungs and force flowers to grow

your pain is the soil that will allow your roots to grow deep

garden my goodness

rebuke thieves that desire to break into the vault of your soul

not everyone is worthy to hold your sin without judgement

...we are at the altar,

honest

yes, broken...

but honest...

These Flowers were held by Broken Vases

⌊ backroads

there exists an eternal sadness;

life after graduation, the survival of warzones

a postpartum anxiety haunting new joy

nostalgic beauty is of the deepest sorrow,

These Flowers were held by Broken Vases

he is faithful in his watch regarding life

inviting himself to unravel out of the quiet,

unsheathing his voice from the corner when loneliness tolls too loudly for just his ears to hear,

he seeks out life to share this mantric hum;

the quiet sting that comes along with the graying of time's hair

he wants to hold her hand, even if her fingers are not as soft as her smile

just to *say* he had experienced spring undress her tulips,

raising his hand, thrusting his shoulders back as to say "i am proud of what i've seen"

my ears have deciphered the static tune of radios from the wind,

this is the song of germinal,

a melancholy meal

These Flowers were held by Broken Vases

yes, free to starve, a freedom of which they fully availed themselves.

These Flowers were held by Broken Vases

L playing with matches

certain scents can cover the odor of sin,

trick you from prayer and have you tiptoeing pass God at bedtime

when sin starts to look more beautiful than dangerous, there should exist a shake in your knees and a pause within your chest

when Love stumbles out of its mind and play dress up with dynamite/do not stand there and watch the explosion

These Flowers were held by Broken Vases

all fires can burn, but there are few flames that are purposed to cleanse

certain heartbreaks must be signed for,

sometimes we must take responsibility even when our hearts cannot find reason

new beginnings usually speak with the tongue of painful farewells

a salute to ships unable to find the float in oceans

a eulogy for lamenting covenants formed by hungry skin and busy yet empty bodies

stop crying at dinner time

eat your supper with gratitude /there are many lessons taught at empty tables

eat your breakfast,

consume the sum of it all

These Flowers were held by Broken Vases

devour your chains and breathe again

and when you exhale do not let go of the lesson you learned

These Flowers were held by Broken Vases

L home

I saw a butterfly denounce its wings once

found itself levitating backwards into the cocoon; the closet

holding its past skeletons

These Flowers were held by Broken Vases

I went home this morning for the first time since I discovered how to smile/ it held the same welcoming as the air after flesh is burned

it was like smelling blood for the first time

ashes are not polite/they will kick down your door and grab hold of your nostrils

my bed woke up and looked at me straight in the eyes/I covered my ears before it had the chance to speak

the clothes on the floor could still fit me but my spirit wouldn't allow it

the scent of smoke whispered from the bathroom and hid behind the hollow eye sockets of the ghanaian masks hanging on the wall,

the door knob crumbled when I tried to leave/now there's a shattered window in that house

These Flowers were held by Broken Vases

extinguished fires have no power, only ghosts

william james lofton-jackson was born in chicago, illinois. at a young age writing always captivated him, but it was during a deployment in afghanistan he discovered the peace and joy it gave him. he is a student at troy university where he is studying political science and anthropology. as a poet, william jackson uses his personal experiences to create narratives that go beyond the borders of traditional storytelling and breaks down the walls of practicality. he desires to shake people from their comfort zones and petition them to live in their truth.

keep up with the author on social media:

instagram: mrjames____

CPSIA information can be obtained at www.ICGtesting.com
Printed in the USA
BVOW06s1926131016

464984BV00010B/206/P